PHILIP BRADY

FORGED CORRESPONDENCES

PHILIP BRADY

FORGED CORRESPONDENCES

New Myths Press
Binghamton, New York

1996

Published by *New Myths Press*
State University of New York at Binghamton, Binghamton, NY 13901-6000
Copyright © 1996 by Philip Brady
ISBN: 0-938621-03-3
Manufactured in the United States of America

Twenty-four of these poems have previously appeared in magazines and literary reviews: Hunger's Painting in *Abraxas*; Three Days from The Black Diaries in *The Belfast Gown Literary Supplement*; How We Got Here in *Birmingham Poetry Review*; Mazembé, The Dream My Father Radios, and Poem Beginning With a Found Line in *The Centennial Review*; Lullaby for Me in *The Chattahoochee Review*; And This is How I Woke in *Cyphers* (Dublin); Internment in *Five Fingers Review*; Baptizing David, and Touring Plague Country in *Footwork*; Flying West from Belfast in *The Graham House Review*; Letter to Ireland in *The Honest Ulsterman*; Letter with Photograph (from Holmen Bentley) in *The International Poetry Review*; Scald in *The Laurel Review*; The Arrival of the Queen of Sheba (in Galway) in *Massachusetts Review*; Mother Superior's Deathbed, The Birds of Ireland, In Pére Paul's Room, and Wiretap in *New Myths: MSS*; Fordham Prep in *The New Virginia Review*; To Catullus in The *Oregon Review*; Letter to America in *Pacific International*; The Cornice of the Skull in *Poetry Northwest*; Letter to Ireland in *Provincetown Arts*; First Born in *West Branch*.

Many thanks to the New York State Foundation for a Thayer Fellowship, to the Ohio Arts Council for an Individual Artists Fellowship, and to the Yaddo Corporation, The Headlands Center for the Arts, and The Millay Colony for the Arts for residencies that helped me during the time I was writing these poems. Special gratitude to teachers and friends who read and suggested revisions for some of these poems, especially Art Clements, William Dickey, William Greenway, John Montague, Steve Oristaglio, Steve Reese, Jerome Rothenberg, and Linda Strom.

The lines from Dante used as an epigraph for *The Dream My Father Radios* were translated by Steve Reese.

All rights reserved. No part of this publication may be reproduced or transmitted in any form or by any means, electronic or mechanical, including photocopy, recording, or any information storage and retrieval system, without permission in writing from the publisher.

Cover artwork 'Epiphany' was painted by Robert Carioscia. Cover was designed by Stuart McCarty.

for Robert Lunday and Robert Mooney
&
i.m. Philip and Anne Brady
1918–1994

> *When at last*
> *In frail old age they stood before*
> *The temple's door and spoke of years gone by,*
> *Philomen saw Baucis shake green leaves around her,*
> *And she herself saw Philomen wear leaves.*
> *Around their faces branches seemed to tremble,*
> *And as bark climbed their lips as if to close them,*
> *They cried, 'Farewell, goodbye -- dear wife, dear husband.'*
>
> —*Ovid*

CONTENTS

I PLAGUE COUNTRY

First Born   1
Flying West from Belfast   4
Touring Plague Country   6
Baptizing David   9
Letter with Photograph   10
Mother Superior's Deathbed   12
Fordham Prep   14
Internment   16
The Cornice of the Skull   18
Letter to Fever   20
Hunger's Painting   22

II THE DREAM MY FATHER RADIOS

Wiretap   29
Scald   32
Three Days from The Black Diaries   34
The Arrival of the Queen of Sheba (in Galway)   40
The Dream My Father Radios   47
In Pére Paul's Room   49
Poem Beginning with a Found Line   53
Lullaby for Me   54
Letter with Photograph   55
Fever, Aphasia   57

III CITADEL OF MOTHS

Letter to America   61
How We Got Here   65
West Point, A Love Song   68
Letter to Photograph (withheld)   70
Citadel of Moths   72
The Birds of Ireland   74
New Age   81
Mazembé   84
Single Flat   92
To Catullus   94
Letter to Ireland   96
The New Life   98

I

Plague Country

*Well, I am still a traveler and I don't know where
I live. If my home is here, inside my breast,
Light it up! And I will invite you in as my first guest.*

—John Logan

First Born

for Anne Brady

The day the four McCann girls were shown Brooklyn
and told that beneath their feet were rivers and tunnels,
another fleet of trams, a whole underground city—
that was the day they realized they'd need me.

They could translate pence to nickels,
knew *mince* meant *raisin*, but one look
at the brickwork, the smoking girders—one look
at their small blue parents inching under the neon
storming the sky, and all but the baby sensed
they'd need an American—rich, educated,
tall if possible.
 But where to find one in the grease-
japped kitchens, in the kiosks, in the velvet sacristies?

On Sundays, Paddies in sloped work caps
leered at McCann's front stoop, greasers
sharked the boulevards, and Jews, garbed as mad priests,
muttered and cawed along the lanes of Prospect Park.
But the only way to get an American was to make one.

Mary was eldest so she tried first, but she barely had time
to squint at the house I'd rent one day
with turrets and stained glass windows opening into pine limbs
before the gardener she married,
whose tenor voice still trills in McCann memory,
died of rare cancer and their girl–child
started to swipe coins and grow black
crooked teeth not like me at all.

Then Betty the prim one entered
the plush mouth of the Savoy movie house
and when she exited daylight

swelled to rubies in her bleary sight, and that night
in her pillow she saw Africa: Bogart's bone deep
American gaze, and she, shimmying in the dream
out of her wool skirt, patting her curls.
                                             All
that summer she peered back into the scum–
white Coney Island surf and then this
Elizabeth, who skipped over sidewalk cracks
and probably steam–ironed her underwear—she
fainted, flailing the flexed waves until
a navvie flung his shoes in after and they
lived like that, fainting and belting each other
while forty years skimmed by like a flat stone and now
she's babbling this fractured tale to me, the sea
meanwhile having shrunk to a damp senile shell,
but she's sure—my aunt—and still furious
that it was me thrashed out of her womb like a knife
(I nod, purr *sure*) and when she stiffens, spits out
that I fecked off the wrong way to some war,
came back someone else, I steal a glance
at my cousin's military snapshot taped to the steel
nursing home bed frame and swear
when it comes to this between myself
and me we'll shoot each other.

Then it was Kay who coaxed a wraith by jitterbugging
her flame fingernails; together they raptured
bars and K. of C. Halls then boogied home to make a me
Christ would mistake for his transfigured twin;
but I'd been craved so many times
it was born smudged—their whelp—padding the threadbare rug
in orthopedic shoes, getting religion,
soiling his musical necktie in the kitty litter.

And that left Anne the youngest who dreamt at first
of turrets and Bogart but finally
it was the dark she loved, mirrored
when she closed her eyes and pulled
a man down into it. That was the travelling then,
she could glide anywhere, the rivers and tunnels
farther than she'd ever seen or thought—no fear,

no need, and when she looked up I was gone
for all the scams they brooded—I'd
slipped back, easy as a hanky through a ring, back
to where they came from as if
they'd never crossed; though it must be
a sliver of me's lodged in the obscure god
who sprays graffiti and puffs black soot
on the crust of Brooklyn, wildly fanning
his worshippers back to life.

Flying West from Belfast

for Anne Davey Orr

*But suicide's
even bigger here
than murder*, you had countered,

and I recall now, waking to a touch,
the tense
architecture of your
profile, burnished

in stained light
of the bombed pub.

But I wasn't dreaming you—

nor spurting, a live
bomb, back
through mother's
and through mother's
mother's womb—it's that far

to touch your beautiful
young clay, the earth
gone
to bring ash when a boy

squinches his face, sobs
yes, and a wing
thunders
underneath my soles. That
was the dream. *Soon*

the stewardess must have said.
We're landing soon, not *son*,

but still I started, felt
the earphone weal my cheek.

How long, you'd sighed,
since I've felt an untrammeled thought.

Touring Plague Country

(cholera epidemic, Ibiaku, Zaire)

      For this snapshot
      I wind myself in cloth
      wax hair & forehead
        step barefoot
        into a bin of salt
   I age, lose my job, starve
         for a week
           & pose
   miles from the camera

            *

   A Swahili Phrase Book:
msungu is white & strange as
    linen & tinned soup
 a flowered dress; two beads
of iodine steep in a china cup

       pombé is beer
Mbuji–Mayi: a city (goat–water)
200 kilometers, 5 days by jeep
   nvisi is animal & meat, *iko*
tayari? is it ready? also your child is sick
leo means now and years ago a woman weeping on a
  flowered dress. *Nvisi* is *mackok* is animal & black

            *

    Back to mat to
    earth
       they lie
    (the dying) & wait
      for the click
they say opens
    cave
      hull
        or hospital room
    they dream in

*

          To pass time
they pass a coin
   mat to mat
              take
  in left palm, kiss
 pass to right & press
between thumb & forefinger
    saying take

*

According to legend
 an army of giants
straddling elephants
descended from mountains
  1000 years ago—
               for them
   war is terrible
because if not killed
 they live 900 years

When they found out
              70
  is quite old
they named this land

    Plague Country

*

A little girl : a key
wasted arms : vast wings
monsieur, how do I stop dying?
   sleep : delay
   bread : bread

*

      Dead night   awake
          I step
   over mats laid straight
                    as matches
open door

no traffic   no road

no moon   no destination

       *

     A man
  bearded, late 30's
  takes my wrist
  & uses my voice
    to say

    cholera is an island
      so no one
    can arrive or leave
        alone

Baptizing David

Last day in camp I took him to the lake.
All summer he'd pled he couldn't swim.
I took him under my arms, he squirmed
and kicked, already drowning. "I love you, love
you," he screamed—the way he'd learned at home
to ward off blows.

The lake was ice calm.
One motorboat cut its engine to fish
half a mile off. I planked him
on the dock, then
jack–knifed up
and started down the ladder, him
stiff on my chest,
my heels feeling for rungs.
I let his cold body slip perfectly still
into the cold lake.
His white hair smelled like hay as it passed.
The scrawny idiot probably would have drowned—
I had to fish him out.

As I watched the head sink
like an egg, blue arms unfolding,
luminous knees rising and plunging,
my cheek still felt the chill
where he put, as he went down
in terror, a kiss.

Letter with Photograph

from: Roger Casement, British Consul to the Belgian Congo
to: E.M.Morel, founder, Congo Free Society; author, Red Rubber. *Liverpool: Congo Free Society Press, 1904.*

        May 3, 1903, Leopoldsville

My dear Morel,

I want to tell you everything I saw
and what the urge to see which brought us here
has done. A blond–haired mercenary
swore (here in my office over drinks)
it was the white men of the Force Publique
massacred Ibiaku. *What shit*
I thought, & listened bored
to the cliched adventures you
journalists dream up—
soup–green jungles, pythons,
leeches, crocodiles *big as big as...*
Africa shrunk down to a penny
dreadful western—if you think
this innocent you've never cut
the figure English clubs so love—
the witness restored miraculous
from parts unknown, well–tanned, prone
to melancholia (let him sigh
as he lights his pipe and some
feckless pillboy will be there
to grip his elbow, thinking how
savage atrocities scarred a noble mind).

The squad crept through mud and vines
and got so close, he said, he could hear
the mamas singing and the pestles
pounding manioc—could even smell
the palm oil and smoked fish.

They were so close he had to twitch
to fret the tse-tse flies that gorged
till stiff as knuckles on his blood
(one slap might warn the villagers).
Finally, at dusk, they started the attack.

Then, before I showed him
the enclosed photograph, he described
and traced in the air
with an ivory & malachite letter-opener
certain cicatrices Captain U.V. instructed
the men to carve on female corpses
to make it look like work of a rival tribe.

I glanced up—for the first time wondered
truth? He rolled his cuff
to show the bites—still fresh.
I followed his malaria-bleared eyes
taking in our British Consulate:
raw teak, framed portrait of the King,
the leaky corrugated tin
that grazes my hair when I stand up.
And all the while
his blue pulse lay there bared for me...to cut
or to detach us—he and I—somehow
from the mutilated bodies pictured here—
the gesture was so natural—
palm up, his forearm hair
the color of the rust stains on this page.

Mother Superior's Deathbed

> *Sing, O barren,*
> *You who have not borne!*
> *For more are the children of the desolate*
> *Than the children of the married women...*
>   ISAIAH

November, 1964, Mission Kibongo, Ibiaku

Every morning now, they flit from Mass
along stone corridors to my window,
like birds you once said hands were. Our first born.
Why should they gawk at this death when they've prayed
untouched through so many others? Just watch them
mewling at me until their wimpled cheeks
redden and they cry, "How did we get here
in this beastly heat?" Ask them a question,
they peck as if to sneak from pocketless habits
a cool coin. Sister Miriam, Sister Monique,
Sister Ildephonse, Sister Marie Therese. Just doves.
Still, they come from our love and we call them
ours. You are the only lover I have ever taken.
But I have other children. Their strange names
and skin like soil or ash came out of a dry season
and I took them to me, built this church
from nothing and tried to make them
ours. My fingers were your daws
digging up fetishes buried behind my back; I sang
your hymns to the roots when they said, "women
must not speak aloud so not to shame
unready seedlings." Even asleep I felt
your covenant spool fiber underground
and the warm earth opening, and manioc,
buffed and thick as candles, yield to hoe.
Come harvest, I didn't heed their wails
or believe the rotten husks they shook
at me were from our garden until I knelt and turned

the chalk–dry ground myself and felt in these,
your hands, the cheesy tubers crumble,
the pledge—to bear fruit—you gave everywhere
here void. But let that quarrel pass.
My bastards know from many a long season
of cholera and starvation who they are.
Fever has been my divination.
When the blond American doctor breathes on me
and pain washes and wrings until I don't know
if his or my eyes water and I forget
myself enough to murmur, "Why..."
then air—for what is air but the dim
glassy eyes I loved and obeyed—
trembles with doubt, and your voice whispers,
"I never knew how not to mold you,
how not to make you what I thought you wanted."
Which means, I suppose, a girl—fussed over,
posed on one leg in an autumn so long past
no one but you and I can conjure. Only we
know the mark on her pale dress
(the photograph's still by my bedside)
is not a leaf or stain (impossible!)
but sunglasses I twirled at a blond boy
I might marry. I might be Miriam giggling
or Marie Therese who puts thumb to muffled ear,
pinky to pink lips miming a phone
to please the only mortal white man here.
Or so you thought. You still don't understand:
virgin or wife, I'd never be like them—
calling you "Father" while you sip life
from a chalice you keep sweet and cool
just to soothe your absence and to feel
you still know after all
what taste, love, touch are.
I see now you were frightened
even then, that autumn. You wanted me
to marry, bear children of my body,
and still stay happy, innocent, and yours.

Fordham Prep

In this, the fire of mid–life one thing
      I know: not if it means
high school again would I agree
        to be reborn.

Between me and hope of a new start
      loom mixers,
wonder bread egg squish,
        and the trapeze

of Anselm's Latin Ontological.
      Not for the school tie,
not for my two sweet, pimple–zippered
        lungs, not for the shine

of all the palm grease on the plastic
      jolt–orgasmic
seats of the Cross–Bronx 20 bus would I
        sign on for a fresh

incarnation. I've a half–life
      left, and after that
I'll whistle fine as dust or sip
        amnesia from a glyphed

gourd or writhe in flames for two
      eternities thank you
before I'll let my ears be
        barbered lopsided,

my cat chloroformed. I'm damned
      if I'll be born again
to end up soaping after gym
        under two drizzly

nozzles one of which turned
        out to be
Dog Baker's dick and so I slammed
        his pasty chest,

wrestled him to the wretched iridescent
        swill, pummelling
the only naked flesh I touched
        in four long years.

Internment

(Ibiaku, two children speak alternately)

When Pére Paul comes Sunday
he brings bananas, fish, and sombé;
he takes some other child.

> On Sunday
> I touch his buckle and he pats my head—
> patron, choose me.

Where does white come from?
The gendarmes caught me hiding in a tree.

> White comes from buildings
> full of pretty things—
> monsieur, choose me, monsieur, choose me.

Shadow's my color,
the moon sheds white
in grains so tiny you can't see.

> When Pére Paul comes Sunday
> there's plenty to go around—
> what did he mean, 'mine'?

So thin the moon
and cold when branches shake
it doesn't shine.

> On Sunday
> he brings me a new name—
> choose me, monsieur, Jean–Paul, monsieur, choose me.

When Pére Paul comes Sunday

I'll touch his buckle and he'll pat my head—
patron, choose me.

The Cornice of the Skull

To lurch, crooning, in moonlight from the pub,
      and wander the Connemara beach,
and grope my tent and collapse, snoring until
      I wake at high tide in the ocean;

to have my car catch fire on the freeway,
      rush begging cups of water, to suffer
the fireman's smirk as he hands me the crisped oil cap
      left unscrewed on the engine block;

to freeze and raise my arms, then sprint into
      deep elephant grass, my skin tingling,
waiting for the bullet from the wild–
      eyed teenage Congolese soldier;

these are the scenes I relive, hope to dream,
      dying, and perhaps just after death,
waving my arms in laughter, saying *yes,*
      from the first I have known this—

or gripping my smashed leg in agony;
      or rocking to music or to loss;
or walking alone, feeling a bird vault
      in my chest or a stone sink—

how I have practiced, stepping through the dream
      awake, the way children imagine
what they most fear, knowing that what
      they imagine best will never be.

How many times have I let my body slip
      out of itself, in dream, the way
my father did? Three times he tried to live
      the dream right to the end—

the first—he almost had it right—just as

        he'd pictured: handing his keys,
his wallet back, waving goodbye, going down
        only to wake, and find himself

still here—but the world dimmed, slivering
        down to a cataracted moon,
and night filling him up until there was
        only a flicker left to die in.

What if no sea or fire consumes, no brain–
        gray bullet flashes once, at last
to blaze the shape I am—a billion instants
        locked in a nerve–comb?

What if I missed it?—and the fields and pond
        and sky outside my window go on
darkening, and words still stiffen even
        as they're fingertipped,

and in my skull, where I drown, or writhe in flames,
        or tense as the blood spurts, a voice
drones on, "I thought you lived, still walked the earth,"
        and I reply forever, "But I do."

Letter to Fever

from: Roger Casement

        July 3, 1903 five weeks east of Leopoldsville

Brother Fever,

So sick, afraid almost to write your name and risk
losing dream–sight of the skiff on Lough Erne,
your strong back at the oars
straining
like Caillebotte's floor scrapers—
although in truth you've never been to Ireland
nor seen a modern painting. Brother
Fever, I think of rubbing your gold back with alcohol
as if distance were varnish I could knead, belladonna
for your eyes, myrrh for love.

Memory must be feeling as your namesake Saint
Augustine writes, for yesterday
when I heard reports that one survivor of a massacre
waited across the river, I remembered
a bruise on your smooth thigh, violet
as a love mark or the sky
over Lough Erne, though truth is
I've never seen your perfect body hurt.
But by the time
I raised myself on elbows, peered across—
no one was there. My fever
felt an absence, refusal to be
witnessed, as if it had been you who bent at dawn
to cup the river water,
then turned your back on tent and dying
fire, returned unseen,
brushing back the whippy branches, toward
some loneliness where even fever can't be brother.
Agostinho, true, malaria

veils my face or yours, but peels at the same time
from my mind's eye the doubt
that what I most fear, I most yearn for.

Hunger's Painting

Safe
        returned to America
some days I stare
        so long across the room
at a sand painting
        sketched on a maize sack
and framed for souvenir

I can almost see
        beneath its gaudy outline
of African lake and sky
        a lake floor
far below
        on fire

Black mud coughs
        watery blue flames
in the mind's eye
        behind the pastel scene
of fishing boats
        and eucalyptus
that hangs on my office wall

Hunger painted it
        and shadowed me down
mud paths past
        palm oil mamas and
pans of matchstick–tiny ndakala fish
        past soldiers squatting on their helmets
and the sassy malachite smuggler
        in Chicago White Sox T-shirt—

Hunger
        a tall man
in green abas–cost
        and ragged polyester shorts

hawked the dream sketch
        still damp
pinching my sleeve
        to coax monsieur l'americain

Now
        daily for me
the Kamalondo marché
        opens:
bundles of ghost
        papaya, squash, and mangoes
blister into flame

while children waft after toy wire cars
        and zip sparks down the leads
to melt the skeleton frames

In the rich
        wet smoke of the Gecomines
miners are finally freed

        by drowning

No one can check
        company boots doled out
or pints of milk
        gulped at the mouth
of the mine to protect bone

I spend whole days
        fascinated
                staring

The jacarandas
        lining the pitted dirt roads
crinkle like paper maché,
the bullet–pocked buildings
        undulate in flames

At night in the bodegas
        batik pagnes

of dancers rouged with fever
    swirl
eerie as manta rays
    to reveal
fiery helix of muscle scorching thigh
    veiny tangerine pulp
of buttocks and hip—

    the lake floor is so hot
the leaves on the painted eucalyptus
    sparkle

Hunger remembered stories—
    how the sun
slanted to deceive the moon
    why mosquitoes whimper
he painted as if light
    blazed from above
to glaze the olive shallows
    and daub
each petal and stalk
    with a live sheen

A woman
    perches
in the bow of a pirogue
    tucked in near fronds

Her torso's a starred almond
    her gaze
drawn by perspective
    to the azure
center
    where a skiff
glides on its own shadow

The traveler's reflection
    curves
sprigs refract
    from the crescent hull
bound for a smudge

                beyond the far shore

The third figure
            bends
into the weeds
            she's found something—
smoked meat or bukari perhaps
            he's left behind

                    Too late—
the boat's already
            inches out of earshot
the long shaft of the oar
            descends
from sky across stick neck
            and knees
straight into coarse water—
            a slash
in Hunger's dream—

            through it
I stare
            at the lake floor
                        and the flames

II

The Dream My Father Radios

I turned to the left—anxious, like a boy...

*intending to tell Virgil, "not one dram
of blood is left in me that does not shake.
I recognize the signs of the old flame."*

But my guide, that sweet father, had gone back.

              Purgatorio, XXX

Wiretap

How could Detective Brady and his perky wife
storm upstairs to enforce lights out
when the bleached blonde perched crosslegged on their sofa
had strangled her two children?
                    Perfectly safe, I moled
between the two top bannister rails, eavesdropped
a spill, a laugh, and something clicking.
She must have sloshed her cocktail,
slipped her high heels off. Soon
muffled sobs, my father's soothing tenor voice, *there there.*
Unthinkable now to slink back to my room, dream murder
mounting the pillowy stairs barefoot.
                              Maybe
the little girl puked up the night of June 23,
or the boy sassed—maybe
it was all finally too much—the late night
waitressing, the Mafioso boyfriends, divorce
in Queens in 1966. Unthinkable—
solitude a thing I could not bear—still is—
internal voices whisper home and twice
they've nearly had me married.
                        The cops had Alice
Crimmons' Ford or something close reliably witnessed
cruising 3:30 AM. Next day,
they chalked one tiny corpse near Kew Gardens. The other—
the girl—lay nesting in the weeds of the World's Fair
for two weeks.
            Once a year,
when my father picks me up at Kennedy, we pass
the silver skeleton Fair globe without a word
for that grim search, the Crimmons trial, the sentence
long since passed. Although his Queens
is a kind of wax museum (at this gin mill
Fuentes outbled Diaz, at this
ristorante Anthony Grace fell) his famous case—
the one they made a book—this one

he hates, because, he says, my mother is not "perky"
and some facts are fudged.
                      True, as the book says,
mick bloodhounds were bent on nailing
that bitch Crimmons—their eyes glazed over when she claimed
she checked the sleeping kids at 3 o'clock. Instead,
they teased clues from her beehive hairdo, they sleuthed
right through the chic shades she donned
for *Daily News* splash pics. Burke was stone stubborn,
Kelly horny to make second grade.
They had the car, they had the coroner
pinning the first death near 2 A.M. Still, they needed
a mole—someone they trusted, someone she would trust.

In *The Alice Crimmons Case*,
Detective Phil Brady's manner is "confessional"—
and after twenty years, a heart attack and stroke,
still is. Clasping his hands,
he hoods the dinner table and the fact
I am a liberal atheist exudes from me
like sweat but seldom does the conversation stray
as far as who he is.
                      Mention the Crimmons case
and something inside him clicks, something is welled in echoes,
something behind his eyes begins to spin
like the old reel–to–reel that hunkered on his basement desk,
state–of–the–art, 1966.
I was too busy jerking off and freebasing
pure heresy at Fordham Prep to eavesdrop cop tapes,
but last month, years after I stormed out the 53-28
screen door swearing *new life,* I spied,
wedged like a scallop on a lost shelf in the basement
of a Berkeley used book shop, the familiar
discounted title. Sobs welled up
in that California cellar, most distant point
in close to as far an orbit around Queens as I'd yet dared—
so far I feared
that if I took two steps, nothing
would pull back.
                      And yet, thumbing that pulp, I realized
my father, a stone Irishman—

a man who croons the Clancy Brothers and bluffs
history—had travelled farther.

What did it mean in 1966 to tape those sobs,
then turn his back on Kelly and Burke—on the Police Force—
and press *erase*?
Queens was a world–rich honeycombed with generations,
it was a safe place for white men
and most women. What did it take
to wiretap—and replay for the defense—loose talk proving
the coroner fudged time of death?
The hack who wrote *The Alice Crimmons Case*
and juiced those sobs to hawk his schlock *exposé*
invents "two sleepless nights" for Detective Brady
before he wakes Alice's sad–sack lawyer.
                                              But when I think
of that ineffectual—or just imaginary—call
I seem to see a door open and my father
take two steps into pure
nothing—but for all my travelling, I'll never know—
and however much I want him not to have to
go on being him, me
being me, I haven't stopped, nor found a way
to tell anyone I love
this story.

Scald

There is a place in far north Canada
where day breaks the color of tea's
first flush, and if you believe
frost, or just a way
of feeling cold, could grip three
generations then maybe
you've been there, or some such place—
the skin–taut road of your own
spine let's say, smooth as
milk spoons—and even if
you're home, even if home
is Berkeley California where sun's
part of the deal, a chill
wisps over you and the brass
rails, the slo–mo Casablanca
whirring fans of your rave café
blur salmon-bright and words
formed and rehearsed on the lush
winding drive up the coast road
freeze in your gorge. In this
Canada, the horizon sharpens. A Canuck
and gaggle of boys issue from a box
house into fierce wind. Work
mills every waking minute;
it is a drudgery I imagine
you can't know—the meals
around you sculpted on pale
china, the service choreographed.
Not that you won't pay. But you
regard the teak, linen, and gold
as if some motif veiled a pistol;
a line blips through your head
like an ad slogan or mantra *life my
life love my own life.* To say this—
you can't yet—but your lover,

the beautiful sleek woman whose voice
has haunted since she phoned,
pregnant, senses it, stays
locked behind the menu's
leather triptych. In the chinky
box house in 1933 a crone
nurses water on a coal
samovar. She is your lover's
grandmother and this, at least,
is her's—this warming of hands before
the day's first task, the day
she accidentally killed her
youngest girl. It's a curse
your lover revealed one lazy
morning months ago, seizing you
from sleep: the scalding
of an infant in the cold
vast waste of Canada. Her curse
then but now, as the waiter
brushes past and the chef
seasons tonight's special
never to have been, you seem
to see the laundry bucket
tense; you feel
close enough to snatch
the child burrowing in the clothes bin
toward sleep, through calico,
toward warmth, forgetfulness.

But when you speak you say *I love
you but I want
nothing to change I want
everything to be just as it was*
and so it is: you're alone, cleaving
blurred redwood cliffs, a bright
wave hissing down through limbs
that shiver like hands feeling
for a child, if you ever risk one.

Three Days from The Black Diaries

> *Afraid they might be beaten*
> *Before the bench of Time,*
> *They played a trick by forgery,*
> *And blackened his good name.*
>   WILLIAM BUTLER YEATS

Typescripts of diaries attributed to Roger Casement were circulated secretly by the prosecution during his treason trial in 1916, but their publication was blocked by the British Home Office until 1959, when they were printed by Grove Press *en face* with Casement's official "Congo Report." The originals have never been released or acknowledged by the British Government.

Their authenticity remains the subject of debate.

    The Congo Report

    Mr. Casement to the Marquess of Lansdowne
    London, December 11, 1903

    My Lord,
    I have the honour to submit my report on
    my recent journey on the Upper Congo.
    I left Matadi on the 5th of June, and
    remained in Leopoldsville until the 1st of
    July, when I set out...

The Diaries

June 5, 1903

I am making up a life
    for myself.
Under strange stars,
    surrounded by dark fens
in the faint glow

    of my cigarette,
        light–headed
it must be

> *My return to Leopoldsville was on the 15th of
> September, so that the period spent on the
> River was one of two and a half months...*

    I have invented
days of butterflies
    how we once struggled up
        Mozamba Hill
up to Bumbuzi

> *during which time I ascended the river and
> its principal feeder, the Lopori, as far as
> Bongandanga, and went round Lake
> Mantumba...*

    & I saw—how many yrs ago?
those birds with long ribbon tails
    (how do they fly?)
& far down below
    spied pelicans, an ibis
& hippos rolling awash
    in the brown river

> *perhaps the most striking change since my last
> journey into the interior nineteen years past
> was the great reduction observable everywhere
> in native life....*

    how we spread
a linen tablecloth on moss,
    feasted
on white bread,
    the only fifth of Jameson's
for 100 miles.
    Agostinho & I,
two noble's sons

> *Communities I had formerly known as large and flourishing centres of population are today entirely gone.*

   it must be
seeing this filth,
    walls, guns—
guns everywhere, only the guns
   not starved—

> *alarming death rate...sleeping sickness....*

I am making it all up:

how we undressed,
   && smoked,
     && slept

1884. Half my life since then.

June 12, 1903

Trade makes a Xian country, Stanley said.

> *"I am N.N. These two beside me are 0.0. and P.P. all of us Y..."*

dashed fat harbormaster 30 francs
to check Morel's claim:

> *"From our country each village had to take twenty loads of rubber. These loads were big; they were as big as this...."*

last month

> *Question: "How much pay do you get for this?"*

3 ships bound "Brussels" listing cargo
"rubber." Two inbound unload "arms."

> *Answer: "No pay. Nothing."*

Trade?

June 12, 1903 (evening)

"Fiba" tonight,
   beautiful,
     very beautiful
kissed many times in street
   & to Avenida

> *I took careful notes of the statements made to me by these people.*

10 francs
   for cigarettes
& very beautiful
   bueno
     diati diaka moke mavebela
fiba
   Fiba X—love

June 14, 1903

today, walked deep into cité
   soon lost
as if
   I had never been

> *...the Government workshop for repairing and fitting the steamers. Here all was brightness, care, order, and it was impossible not to admire...*

here

> *nearby, within a hundred yards...*

   then, in the maze
of mud paths,
   found myself

at the very hut
   where first met
Agostinho.

      three mud huts which serve the purpose of the
      native hospital...

   shocked, impossible
but thought I saw
   him

      I found seventeen sleeping sickness
      patients, male and female, lying in the
      utmost dirt...

& I touched
   a brown shoulderblade
on bare mat.
      a man fell into the fire while in the last,
      insensible....

   God help me—
wanted to lie down with him.

But when I bent down

      All seventeen were near their end...

   it was
a stranger—he flinched
   like a raw wire
screamed "the white will eat me"
   shocked, both shocked

      and on my second visit two days later
      I found one of them lying dead in the
      open...

   then I looked up
through peeling thatch,
   saw

first black rain clouds of the year
   & recognized
      this tingling,
  this fever:

my malarial spleen proves
  I was here.

The Arrival of the Queen of Sheba (in Galway)

1 BLACK PROTESTANTS

> *with me whack fol le do fol le diddly eye dee day*
> *"THE GALWAY RACES"*

Song comes from a place, means what the place does. Flushing: noun & verb. "G" not pronounced as in Long Island nor dropped like Brooklyn.

The place: a cabinet Hi Fi. Press the last key on the right it thumps & sticks. Two racing stripes light green; the Hi Fi thrums.

The place singing comes from is the right lobe. The LP fits in the left drawer. I crouch before the dashboard, ear to scruff of speaker, and hear four electric pulse beats: *buff buff buff buff.*

Father's downstairs. Mother's lip curls and her foot stamps time. "Up the Rebels!" says her jutting chin.

I rock. On hands & haunches back & forth, haunch to heels & palm to rug, speed adjusted to song.

Father screams up, "Turn that noise down."

Mother screams down, "Narrowback!"

Understanding and guile share the left lobe. I understand *moonshine, porter, stout, poteen; sassanach* is my hissed curse; I am *langers; peelers, pishogues & fenians harry & cock; I rove; I stand & deliver—fore & aft, a bloody briny daft shoneen* with an eye peeled for a *crubeen* or a *colleen,* a *dragoon,* an *omadon,* a *quay.*

Soon I begin to understand Gaelic & *ad fiason la port laragot, fa dow, fa dee, fa le god–e–lum* is as clear to me as *with houls ime shoos ame tows peepin troo siyin shinnymarinkadootaloffin ould jonny doo.*

Foreign, slippery, forbidden to play in snow, Leo Sarkissian lives next door in a house that smells like sour milk. When he knocks, I turn the Hi Fi up.

> *And there were half a million people there*
> *of all denomination*

> *The Catholic, the Protestant,*
> *the Jew & Presbyterian.*

"Ha!" snorts Leo. "That shows how stupid you are. Presbyterians are Protestants—it's the same thing."

"They are not! They're not just Protestants, they're Black Protestants. Black is Gaelic for Colored," I explain.

Father stomps upstairs.

"Mr. Brady, Mr. Brady," Leo whines. "Presbyterians aren't Colored, are they, are they?"

Father's knuckle–red eyes disappear behind his nose. He grips an armchair and flops down crooning, "Colored, of course they are." He sniffles and sits up. "Black as tar body & soul."

Leo burps, then jumps up just in time with me after him down the stairs. He squirms through the screen door and I grab, but he breaks loose, racing down the street, squealing "Jesus Jesus Jesus" to slow me—knowing Catholics bow.

2 THE DISCOVERY OF FLUSHING

> *But the sea is wide and I cannot swim over*
> *nor have I wings so I could fly*
> "CARRICKFERGUS"

It was my younger brother who first discovered we were not living in Galway. Of course, the evidence was overwhelming: gutted buildings, barbecues, centerfolds, sneakers, baseball diamonds, father's heart attack, subways, black people (not on this block but on certain ash–gray stoops nearby), the service revolver Uncle Ed discharged into his mouth, the unavailability of donkey carts, the weird way nothing smelled of turf, traffic in which Chevy Impalas cruised as gracefully as Astin–Martins and the absence of Astin–Martins from the traffic. How strange I never realized we had been living in Flushing all our lives until one Sunday morning during a commercial when, tearing loose from my headlock, my brother screeched, "Stick it up yer ass!"

Soon I found out the friends he brought home, Eddie McGirr & Hector McCluskey, had shadows named DeChico, Greenberg, Diaz. They hung out in the Bohack parking lot, smoking pot and taunting passersby in a way that, had we been living in Galway, would have brought the hairy knuckles of the parish priest down sharply on his skull and left my brother a sorry fugitive in Connaught.

Daily he added proofs of his discovery: obscene cloud formations, vinyl, acid–rock. He grew as I diminished until his Flushing overwhelmed even the fiction of having been born in Galway, and our parents, whose Irish birth occurred so long ago that the accent had worn off, had to settle for being born in Brooklyn.

Demonic, implacable, soon he became my older brother. He pointed and the phone rang off the hook; sirens wailed in the bathroom; ferocious Bronx girls be–bopped topless on the coffee table while Father & I danced like bobble–heads and Mother wiped neat ovals over & over on a greasy dish. He preened before us in a zoot suit, hair flecked with platinum, diamonds guarding each plump knuckle, while we bowed, bumptious & simian, like the Paddies of Victorian *Punch* cartoons.

And all this simply because a slight tardiness in development let my younger brother discover we were living in Flushing before I did.

3 HERACLITUS BOYER

> *If they have to be the Flushing Dodgers, they might as well be the Los Angeles Dodgers.*
> WALTER O'MALLEY, late owner of the Brooklyn Dodgers

Everything changes and remains the same. Our souls sleep and when we die they come to life.
So Heraclitus, and so I understood, halfway between WWII & now. Because things grow as they grow less real, the World's Fair; Shea Stadium has miles of parking.

Inside, at the very rubber, the soul of Koufax's furious body —placid, artful, perfect–in–detail (toe pointed to crotch of diamond behind first, glove curled swanlike overhead) swoons in Jerry Koosman. Armspeed is generated water; the pitch is Koufax's wistful soul.

And I, left–handed, right–brained, fling a spalding at the stoop to pry Tom Seaver from his all–star soul. An operation requiring that one time, once only, & under game conditions, I match, closer even than his own body, the motion the soul makes while he takes the sign, brings arms up to & behind head, pivots, tucks & unleashes speed laced with perfect form at a target which is his character & his fate.

Such has been done. *When men die there awaits for them what they neither expect nor even imagine.* Pee Wee Reese transmigrates into Bud Harrelson; Ron Hunt has Jackie Robinson's spleen; Ed Kranepool is Gil Hodges but can't say so because Hodges is still there—notice Gil's vacant eyes.

Flushing has practiced for fifty years and finally one weekday morning the airbrakes of a truck on Roosevelt Avenue sigh f#; the wind gusts the pages of the late edition of the *Daily News* at the Main Street Newsstand to the obits page; a blond hooker on Northern & Astoria lights her second Marlboro; there is an accident on Francis Lewis between an Italian grocer in a blue Ford & a Chinese woman in a red Chevy in which three eggs break; a cop snoozes at his desk in the circus of the 111 precinct; a finger bleeds in Fresh Meadows; everywhere breakfast pop-tarts pop perfectly timed with the way it's dreamt by the oversoul of Brooklyn (which is so exhausted from dreaming it is Warsaw, Peking, Sicily, Galway, Tsarsko Selo & Jerusalem the dream fabric is stretched to transparency and could last only a few more nights at most anyway) and the soul of Brooklyn passes soundlessly into Flushing.

No one knows the date.

The lord who is oracle of Delphi neither speaks nor is silent but gives a sign.

There is a multitude of signs. Puerto Ricans take over the car wash on Prospect Place; the Hasidim riot; Aunt Mary is mugged three times in broad daylight on Flatbush Ave; Walter O'Malley lies still in the City of Angels.

4 GREEN BERET

> *And a soldier he always is decent & clean*
> *In the finest of clothing he's constantly seen,*
> *While other poor fellows go dirty & mean*
> *And sup on thin gruel in the morning.*
> "ARTHUR MACBRIDE"

There is a terrible penalty for not knowing where you are, so terrible it can only be endured or witnessed in castles where people lived hundreds of years ago.

For a snapshot, I pose on the ramparts of Fort Ticonderoga. My right hand pats a cannon; the left cocks a plastic pistol to my brother's head. My mouth puckers to make the explosion sound.

Miles below, the highway threads through meadows; the vista stretches to pine forests from which Ethan Allen's Green Mountain Boys emerged to storm this fort.

The breeze blows the stale car wrinkles from my shirt. In the cannon's touchhole is an iron spike—replica of the one Ethan Allen drove in. Tour guides sport blue colonial tails or buckskin breeches; Father flicks ashes into a tri-cornered hat ashtray.

Green Mountain Boys didn't need costumes or decorations or history or even bodies that could be clothed & captured. On May 10, 1775 they climbed sheer walls, surprised the guards and overcame the fort without a struggle. Thinking I'm them, thinking I'm one of John Wayne's Green Berets, I drop, when no one's looking, down the blind hatchway marked *Keep Out.*

I let myself down gently, my heels feeling for rungs. A lantern hangs from a peg, softening the dark. I feel my way down the stone hall to an oak door marked *Barracks,* where twenty cots stand in perfect rows, and under each a pair of vinyl boots. Next door's the *Magazine*: muskets stacked like matchsticks, barrels with *Gunpowder* scrawled in charcoal.

At the half-door marked *Headquarters* my heart jumps. In eerie light, a figure in frontier costume points a buckskinned arm past a parchment battle map, splashed red.

I follow the painted yellow gaze of the wax Ethan Allen to a cave set off from the main tunnel by iron bars. One prisoner lies on a hammock, his hair half hiding his sallow face. The inscription reads, "Revolutionary discipline was strict. Offenders were flogged and given a bullet to bite so they would not scream." A mannequin stoops over the straw-caked floor, revealing scarlet lines scored on his wax back.

And who is he? A Green Mountain Boy born in open air, convinced by his father that the fort was revolving faster & faster, flaking off bits of stone that would enchant root & tree, elk, bear, his own lithe body, and that to protect the old ways he would have to belly up slick walls and kill the foreigners who want to turn green mountains red. He must take their places so no one else will come, and when he fails to understand, he will endure a terrible penalty and will not be permitted to scream.

5   THE ARRIVAL OF THE QUEEN OF SHEBA (IN GALWAY)

> *I dreamt it last night that my true love came in.*
> *So softly she entered, her feet made no din.*
> *She moved away slowly, and this she did say,*
> *'It will not be long, love, till our wedding day.'*
>   "SHE MOVED THROUGH THE FAIR"

  The vast lunchroom is silent. All heads bow; breastbones press contritely to the backs of chairs; silently, lips trace prayer—first "Grace" then an "Act of Contrition" for provoking Sister Benedict into the sin of wrath. 560 rubber chair feet gurgle over tile; 140 lunchboxes engraved with Roy Rogers, Joan of Arc, Heidi, Superman, JFK, The Three Stooges, The Choir of Seraphim, Nancy Drew, Bozo, Zorro, Rin Tin Tin, Yodelling Swiss Children, Your Friend the Dentist & His Apple Assistant, Dick Tracy, Mother Goose, & Lassie unlatch. Wax & aluminum foil crackle.

  When the Queen of Sheba appears for the first time, she lifts with dainty fingers a jelly sandwich to her luscious mouth. I stare so hard she seems to tremble like a slinky or a TV on the fritz. Later, in the playground, a giddy ring of warlocks circles her, chanting

> *Sister Benedict's on the roof.*
> *It's getting dark what will she do?*
> *Now she tries her wings to flap,*
> *She dives to give...*

and before they chime "Maureen a slap," Declan McCormack darts into the fire of her presence, steals the sneaker off the arched foot of the weeping Queen of Sheba, and wings it over Betsy Riordan's clumsy reach into my outstretched arms. I catch it between palm & neck. The plastic lace tips lash my eye, but I squeeze the token, slender as a zucchini, and gallop away, rubbing the sweaty sole to ear & cheek. When I turn back, I see the Queen has stopped crying long enough to spread her jacket underfoot. There she stands, her school jacket turned inside–out, the cotton lining fresh as snow around her bird–slim ankles.

She has appeared many times since then.

I know it's the Queen of Sheba if it hurts in the teeth, if I sweat to remember what never happened, if even when I'm touching her tanned breasts, the dark purple aureoles between my fingers, my ear to her jewelled belly, it feels as if any moment there might be no one there at all.

I know it's the Queen of Sheba when the pain is pure & distant, like the music of Handel or O'Carolan—the pain that precedes me and comes after.

Once, as I strolled between tables at a family party, humming an air, Aunt Betty gasped and reached up to me with her bony hands, her eyes suddenly lucid.

"Mother," she whispered, "and you dead all these years."

I never met my grandmother, but "The Arrival of the Queen of Sheba (in Galway)" is, my senile aunt still thinks, the tune we hum.

The Dream My Father Radios

Tonight I am Herb Score, his rush
of butterflies, his high
goose kick, fierce pivot
and release. The sky
over first one instant is a blur
of grandstand crepe;
I can do anything, I struck out 238
my rookie year. Then the sharp
crack of the bat, my eye smashed
by the line shot and I
wake, as always, flinching
from your dream—the nightmare
you send clear across the continent
from the sour bed you lie in, in your boxer shorts,
afloat in the TV glow of late news, dozing off.

Some nights I'm Wrong–Way Corrigan,
barnstorming due East to California;
MacArthur fading out; Louis
KO'd. Since you can't talk to me
except to rant about Iran, unions, millionaire
coke fiends—your beautiful white hair and tenor voice
aflame with hate for the dissolving world—each night
you broadcast some nostalgia–sweet disaster. Your heart's
a sleek black fire–escape portable,
blue melodies wind through its whisky–amber
fantasy where every moment shimmers till
even strangers mourn together,
the harmony more than making up for what was lost.

But me, I want
the rush of butterflies when
Score's wool tunic blazoned *Indians*
bunches my thick shoulders
and the ball between forked fingers
feels like the pommel of a lightning bolt—

I want to dream my life
released in one pitch—a smoking seed, unhittable—
while false regrets and goodbyes
evanesce,
leaving whatever self is in the pulse.

But even in that yearning
I hear the crack and crumple to the ground. Bits of sky
break through the bloody webbing of my Spalding glove
and you appear—a weepy vulture or angel
of disaster—you crook me in bristled wings, dreaming
me back past speech contests, sophomore pranks, first
kiss into the half–life where everything's lived twice.
Let go, I whine. I'm not afraid of blindness or pain
because you can go on. Herb Score did—
cranking his herky–jerky windup through eight seasons
of .500 ball, each kinked delivery cramping
the stomach where tonight I had butterflies even
if he never again felt them. He's still
alive somewhere, selling insurance maybe, or scouting bush
leagues, but in the radio dream world he's transformed
to the cliché veteran in boxy suit
boozing at the club, slurring to girls, *I shtruk at tooth–
thudiat one year.* In the foyer,
his rookie picture hangs, autographed, *your pal,
Herb Score* and under it, you stand,
a young man now, kneading my taffy biceps the way
you did after I got bombed in little league big games.

We live it all again, father and son
embrace and mourn together, watching
the beefy ghosts glide through the light.
The maitre'd greets them warmly,
clasping each ruby–studded wrist,
Welcome, Mr. Capone. I love those talkies, Mr. Flynn.
Every night one more and soon you too will enter through
the narrow door and let me go; only at daylight
will I wake, remember, and think *wait, come back.*

In Pére Paul's Room

Mission Kibongo, Ibiaku

A woman stripped
        here in this room
                you start
again the tale
        your hands
                lock in your lap
your stiff back rocks
        forward on starched sheets

                her wail
rings here from thirty years ago
        the bed springs squeak
                the jags of wallpaper
have heard this so many times
        they blur
                in your mind's eye
to smoke of rag torches
        teak masks & raffia skirts
                close in
on the tin tray
        the fruit basket
                lights up with
curiosity & smoke
        so fierce
                you blink &
stutter once
        again
                she stripped
to the waist

        it was a funeral here
                thirty years ago
you came to this lake to sanctify
                a heathen ceremony

father of light—father who gives bread
        you piped
                your memorized Swahili text
while drums beat & torches closed on
        your fear so intense
                you felt naked
underneath your stiff
        brocaded chasuble

                you did not understand

the wail
        that pierces
                thirty years
something to do with *light*
        you don't know
                what miracle or sin
reveals her now—
        her breasts
                flapping against her—
        the paps
heavy as mud on a spade tip

        I watch
                your palms stick
to the glass of syrupy wine
        the mangoes
                light up
photographs of relatives long dead
        watch you
                rock forward
steady your palsied fingers
        as she stumbles
                near, you
try to pierce
        with a tin knife
                the skin
of an iodine–soaked pulp &

        she wails
                a tongue you did not

            understand
                        as the blade hops
                                    & I take
            the papaya from your hands & slice

                        daydreaming breasts
                                    sunned for me
            in my own country
                        sweet taste
                                    of California wine
            & belly lint &
                        fur, undoing
                                    a lace bra—or
            breasts glimpsed on a beach
                        or slicking nude
                                    through blue smoke
            to the tick tick tick of film strips while

                        gently, you release
            the neck
                        of the tottering
                                    carafe, your hands
            appeal to me as if I saw
                        her slink smoke–dark into the room
                                    I turn
            & crack a rib of the venetian blind

                        outside
                                    the tended jacarandas
            flame, *light up* she must have cried
                        meaning enlighten
                                    you insist

I squint at fierce light glinting off the lake & now

            you rise, you
                        shuffle toward me
sure she tears a flowered blouse out of the wallpaper
            for you, for
                        you alone, your one
convert in this blinding sun to wine,

                beads, chasuble
                        light, her ghost voice
        rises in your throat, your fingers reach
                toward me to take a halved
                        papaya
as if across real distances

Poem Beginning with a Found Line

My parents and Monet exist as alcoholics in the garden.
The men are flared brush strokes; the clouds
Monet has thinned into my mother's summer dress
mute shifting light. All morning
the three blur; they feed on surreal bees
as big as tumblers, the stings still potent. And if
the painter, giddy, twirls my father's eyebrows
a grave iodine, dabs fright, gaunt as a key,
into my mother's face, it is nothing
to spend afternoons huddled under the cobra–petaled lilies,
shivering, weeping all three together, while
pain, which they experience as storm,
beats down. Evening, soothed,
they stroll through gentian and coltsfoot to the pond's edge,
while last light silts the water. Dusk
and Monet believes again this is his masterwork; that's why
he stays; to be inside the painting unscrews
something inside him; tonight it is the color
of zinc, and he messes it, idly as a child
his meal, into the moss, the wormwood and angelica
whose absence blots, absorbs him. Or numbed
by every bloom that swells into a face then fans
back into garden, it may occur
to him there is no art, no other life than this:
looping a grief–blue pool, propped by a pair whose ribs
feel cold as needles, but even so, he's terrified
they'll leave. And as for them—whom I've found here—
finally I tap coarse, palpable midnight
for their eyes, trusting this dark, where
nothing that has ever happened happens.

Lullaby for Me

On the days I am not my father I wake more slowly.
The light swells and I spiral upward gently,
though padding to the bathroom I'm still dizzy
and once I lurched back to the bedroom
chewing my toothbrush just to see
if the face holding the mirror hostage
matched the drool stains. But most mornings
I rise and dress like him and the day
is the color of sand or not and I perform
the acts of speaking and occasional
light lifting and the drinking
of scotch afterward and the undoing
of zippers prefatory to sleep
all in a flash—all done
in advance at the moment of waking,
and on these days there is no need
to die or to become a strange god
who holds a severed, waking head by the hair
at arms length, or to acknowledge him
if seen in the office or train, and I sink
without fear my bag of flesh might burst
though it rock and tipple alone or in
someone's arms like a fish digging.

Letter with Photograph

from: the Reverend W. Holmen Bentley, Chevalier de l'order Royal du Lion
to: Roger Casement, Leopoldsville

April 2, 1903 Mission Kibongo, Ibiaku

Dear Sir Roger:

I thank you for the tar
but rain—if sheets torn
from gray heaven, pounding
for three months can be called
rain—has rotted thatch
beyond repair: we'll need
tin if ever we're to sleep.
Friend, my gums bleed. I burn
and freeze, flies
sting, and I've gone deep,
hours, whole days at a time
into that place where pain
brims over and I lie
just numb. It's enough
to make me wish with the old
gnostics: let there be no
body, just eyes and lush green
vegetable soul. Let the eyes
flourish. Forest and sky. Sight
so keen that when a bird
darts from its perch I don't
track flight but watch
the shape that was
flash up and
crumple in bright air. It's fever—
I know—both worlds in me
shivering. But in
these photographs, which no doubt
you've stared and wondered at

before reading this dispatch—
which world? I see you,
friend, the way I see
those birds, the way
I still see in my mind a field
of hacked flesh. Smoke
led me there but what made me
take photographs—then nurse
them visible in the chinked dark
of my hut—is the thought
I'd die inside not knowing
(and you, here twenty years
to my three months, must
know) if it's in
them—the ones we've come
to save—or in the air—
this contagion
that makes men kill
and cut Christ's cross
in flesh.   And so I send
this with the Roi de Belge
and Korzeniowski—himself
a well man last month when he
unloaded tar but now,
returning from further
up the river, so sick
that if by miracle he survives
and you receive from him
my question, you'll have touched,
as I felt touching his,
God's trembling hand.

Fever, Aphasia

There, frost tinted windows, speechlessness, white hair,

> here—fever, dawn pinking wood blinds, mouse gray
> sleeves under my eyes, and the eyes
> themselves swelled scars from when
> my body shone, woad-blue.

There, hum of hospital light, the crumbling in sleep,

> in me, a needle spins,
> demagnetized.

Scrubbed tile, soft blip of screen
far off, where my father fumbles his striped cotton blouse

> and dawn is *yearn*, is *fire, fear*
> so strong I twitch awake

arms shriveled, his fourth stroke in a year
silencing his nerves like stubborn lightning

> alone in my first skin as if I were
> self–made

and his hands, clumsy as gloves, unknot the cloudy string

> sole, incandescent—

and he turns, rises from bed, levitates to stand
in his sleep–body shivering

> dawn in my raw throat
> blazing through cracked lips

in the body he himself is now: his father—
there, in the passageway he glimpsed first thirty years ago

      as if fever were speech—
      kissing the flaming coal sky

when his father faltered into stroke
stuttering Phil—his name, his son's, mine, and he—the son—

      in rapid babble, blistering the world,

my father—gathered silent under wings of his white trenchcoat
his wife, son, peering into the passageway where now

      here, far off,

he fills, gull-white, the shape he glimpsed, he passes back

      each word searing to cinders

his keys, his wallet, cigarettes, as he once took
his father's, and they lay, warming where they're named.

III

Citadel of Moths

Here are some fragments of my hammer which I broke against a wall of jewels.

—James Wright

Letter to America

from: Sam Mayoyo, Assistant au Gerant de l'Hotel International
d'Immoquateur, *Ibiaku*
to: David Reed, *author of* 111 Days in Stanleyville, *New York: Readers Digest Press, 1965*

May 10, 1964, Ibiaku

David,

The Simba hunters have been hunted
deep into the forest, or shot down
by Belgian and American troops—here
on streets visible from this cot.
Two weeks ago the city
was a conflagration and today
biz–niz hisses through the burnt marché
and in the shrugs and smiles
that make for me three languages
comprensible. Biz–niz mon cher
means more than watching ivory
shipped out, guns shipped in—
it's in the sheen of flamboyants,
bare feet on paved boulevards;
it's in the fact and myth
of the big river. In fact—
block out the marché and any view
from this Red Cross circus tent
could sell postcards of the model
Africa Belgian and American guns
protect. Mon vieux, it was this
image—not just enemy bullets—
that the Simbas melted with their
fetishes—fourteen year-old boys
rigid with forest magic chanting mai,
mai, crones painted invisible—
however primitive, their power

held this city for three months.
So now, if the fantasy of glass
skylines and cool squalor
I ogled my six months in America
touches me, it touches
for the first time hungry to feel
what I've passed through
(or what has passed through me).
I feel it in the glances
nurses cast, in your
aerogram I have magically
received, in the delight
with which the Belgian doctor
unwraps chocolate and unfolds
Tribune photographs
of corpses sprawled before
the Art Deco facade of my
Immoquateur—and
it is this—this
touch—more than my own
suffering and the suffering
I have witnessed—that confirms
for them and perhaps also for me
that this is history. And so
you would like news now I am
history. And I would send—
except of course in a disaster
area there are no stamps.
Stamps, and the French cut
of my trousers, my clipped accent—
when the rebels came I feared
their magic would read in these
the absences I could not help
but conjure: cars
steaming on the Triboro,
the roar of the bright
cliffs of Yankee Stadium.
These three months I've walked
barefoot, head down, terrified
the Simbas who imagined
radios in gold teeth,

microphones in silver
belt buckles would
detect in me the inner eye
that followed—as General
Olenga proclaimed a New
Congo—your image
promenading the bleachers
in your tie-dye Boo-Boo,
while I shrugged, played Africain—
stripping my shirt to mock
your pink skin, swallowing
hot dogs smiling *ummmm—
tastes just like snake.* The fact
I once called my own country
a Bronx Zoo without bars, that I
winked at white chicks, thanked
the subway maps you sketched
to keep me safe from American
black men—wasn't this
visible? But no one noticed.
In the New Congo, it seems,
I am common as dirt except
my feet are soft. You ask just
who the Simbas are—and for you
in New York they must seem
the flowering of some rage
planted in Africans
when the *flamboyants* took root,
or if not that then super-
stitious cannibals. You
want to know the truth
firsthand—you demand:
which? My friend,
I only know these three months
every day I've imagined death:
a Simba rifle leveled at my face.
I saw in the mind's eye
the trigger squeezed—but felt
no pain—instead, I heard
a camera click, and stepped
outside myself savoring

absence as the blood spurted
and the body fell. But that day
two weeks past when the mercenary's
bullet struck me there was nowhere—
nowhere to go but down.
I did not glimpse
the paradise of Yankee Stadium,
nor hear the loudspeakers the newspapers
claim blared from burning roofs
in Swahili, French, and English:
We will make fetishes of the hearts
of the Belgians and Americans.
We will dress ourselves in the skins
of the Americans and Belgians.

How We Got Here

Near sleep, 3 A.M. and I descend—
    still sprawled out on your den's plump couch,
still sipping scotch from Waterford cut glass
    watching you grin; without a sound I fade
toward rainy landscapes we once hitched through:
    Galway, Listowel, while the intercom hums waves
of your wife's and children's safe, unbroken sleep
    and beyond sliding glass doors
rain slicks lawns and avenues stretched tense
    as cellophane on bulldozed farms.

Awake, we play at being brothers: *get a job!*
    get real! you roll your eyes
while I karate-chop your neck and cadge your ties
    for dates and interviews
though you are younger. Even our past is staged:
    the day I played dead, laughter
under acid stars, the cops flashlighting pot seeds
    in our Cougar's dash—
all night I've waved highballs big as lampshades
    and slurred over the path that brought us here.

But now my gaze turns in, and *sea-green Connemara rocks*
    swell in my booze-lit skull
where I pose you, sixteen, in ripped jeans,
    on lonely jigsaw roads in stinging rain.

Even a child, I was enthralled by rain—
    the way it let me be
two places (here and lost in a jewelled trance)
    so the year I drifted east across the sea
crones tilting like herons in the wind,
    kerns tottering stotious out of myths,
seemed nearly real—but you, my link, my pretty punk—
    breezing in to check out where we'd be
if there were no such place as Brooklyn—

    you were a tanned brass cocky trip.

So I set you up on our quick tour
    to flag the Astin–Martins, small as bumper–cars
while I crouched round a bend and smirked
    at faces gargoyled by streaked windscreens—
gnomes gaping at you from a lost world Yanks evolved from.

    I see it all as if
I'm underwater and I barely hear you mutter
    from the surf *live now* while I dive down,
past shell–bright roots of scars, cells blowzy
    with booze, and nightmares
translucent as lime jellyfish. I swim
    for somewhere we're the same:
our charged, whorled source. But it's no use.
    The way you grin, the way
you arch your back and stretch blond, muscled legs
    on the bronze rug—why
we can't be brothers! I can't even blame genes
    or a wrecked home
for paunch, thin hair, or for this need
    to talk myself and everyone else blue.

You rise and yank me up and hook my arm
    to stroll pocked asphalt streets
under spent clouds. *I'll tell you what,* you say
    and since it's you
finishing the story I began near sleep—
    the tale I've wound like a starred cloth around
the years we've lived in separate time zones—
    I'm jarred awake
to hear a car I don't remember slowed
    to swallow you, then gunned
past me, the driver flashing hand–signals
    (Shakespeare in sign–language)
to which I gave the finger. And since it's me
    listening there's no need
to describe the dreamscape he sped through,
    or his look: nose veined, eyes rheumy,
as he skidded to a stop, twisted at you

and you pump the doorlatch—miles down that road
       and here, returning home
as dawn's first glint streaks cold houses—
       and I'm caught—as you were then—
in a clammy grip pulling me toward the dark
       you've locked inside these years. There
a ghost seals the windpipe; I see him
       through glass breakers drown
your mouth, fish between your legs until
       you squirm loose, writhe
and splutter to the surface of the sky
       to make your way as far as you could go,
needing to break from him, to break from me.

West Point, A Love Song

There was a miniature room inside my mind
with louvered windows and two bunks clicked into the wall
and I would go there sometimes
when a nun swooped down or grinning camp counselors
fingertipped me through the sawdust terror
to propose a slow dance to the prettiest third-grader.
                                                                          There
I'd tuck the safety-pin tight cot without alarm clock
whether or not I woke from dreaming
forbidden climbing to the roof, little at first,
just to see, and older like a toothsome spider
eking up the ladder to moon Janice Molino's
heart-shaped window pane.   I was eleven,
shiny as tin then and could fit often in the matchbox
studying from four to seven silently an oval
on the institutional desk. When dawn
clicked lights-out red spots danced and taunted
my shut eyes: I fought them with a sword—a plastic
saber thrusting. Demons surrounded
me and my plumed tri-cornered hat refused to die
even when the waves rose on the sea and I saw
for the first time fear in a man's eyes.
                                              I marched in file
to anti-curiosity class, to sun-boxing, IQ
stood for intense quiet, I stood for
hours at attention, the parade ground turning spokes
inside my mind where I kept dry, full-dressed, buttoned
under high school initiation golden showers,
crying and punching the big striped boxer trunks.

I loved West Point.
Meals clicked out at five on metal trays: Precisely segregated
peas, mashed potatoes without chives, two leaves of beef
I ate with eyes glued to Star Trek in despair.

And I'd have stayed I think and lived there
even after risking *Air Zaire*
and bouncing off a palm–oil singing smoked–fish goat truck
and hiking thirty–two jungly klics
to rendezvous, exhausted, finally at the end
of a twenty–five year rope—I
might have graduated, pure as the lead
sad miniature soldier, lame, hopelessly involved
with the porcelain ballerina I still melt for
                                                        if,
when I that sand–grit day thought *love,*
your blear–red eyes hadn't answered *yes.*

Letter to Photograph (withheld)

from: E. Morel
               July 9, 1903, Liverpool

Casement,

Although we've never met I feel
I know you. Not as everyone
who hears your exploits does—not as
the incarnation of vague yearnings. Even
our taciturn Korzeniowski can't help
spinning yarns about you sauntering
through unspeakable wilderness with nothing
but a native porter and two
brindled dogs, to emerge
months later, he says—
gaunt, well-grimed—but flourishing
your Irish blackthorn stick as if
just back from a stroll through Phoenix Park.
The Congolese call you Monafuma
he informed me, which can mean
Noble's Son but also in vernacular
Girl's Rod. How instructive to know
Africans pun, he said, and winking, slid
this photograph across my desk:
A tall, spare man reclining
in a rattan chair. Yes, I know you.
I've never been south of Liverpool
still I recognize the kind that manages
to keep his trousers pressed and
beard well-trimmed in Africa.
Years before your like cut checks
to my crusade against the tyrant
I rose to the rank of dock clerk
by my fists. It was dim light,
but I didn't flee to Africa, instead
I taught myself Engels and watched

in disbelief my brothers
live like beasts. Finally I understood
the cyphers I logged each day—
winchesters shipped out, ivory
and rubber shipped back in—meant
bugger the adventure—everywhere
was just the same as here.
And knowing, do you think I stare
into the limpid eyes beneath your
country gentleman's slouch brim
with admiration? It is my manuscript,
not Conrad's fancy, that will fix you
in time's frame. *Red Rubber*
is pure fact: I assure you
of the utmost accuracy to the last
detail: even the rubber trees
that illustrate each chapter
were traced from horticultural manuals;
the India ink Goliath Beetle
planned for the frontispiece was drawn
faithfully to scale by my own hand.

Citadel of Moths

The thrill was such, the whisky
and fast talk, that when
some booze-hound shoved, my brain-
stem clenched and I seemed
to glare from my grandfather's eyes,
grandfather Joshua, named
for his crazed blood:
my blood too, but thinned,
cooled in the body of his son,
my father, between us, body
lovely and mysterious as a night
lake fringed with teal lights.

And it was the Joshua in me
who pivoted
in the raw burled muscled
sawdust, snarled, gave the drunk
two choices: run or fight. Joshua
once tattooed Durocher in sand-
lot ball they say and swaggered
home boil-red each night
crooning, "Where the hell is
Mame?"

But when my wild hooks bunched
the beige sleeves of my raincoat
and I crumpled, a parched heron,
to the tar-streaked floor I
glimpsed, on the ringed wall
of my inner skull lit
by flashed sparks of each
intimate, glancing blow,
my grandfather—his paper
yellow forehead, the fin shape
of his feet twitch and go still
in the hospital
under my father's gaze.

But I can't be flayed
alive, and who, sober,
would be cracked
and beaten just to be remade
as a specter of fire
sizzling in rain?

Open me now, childless,
fatherless; you'll see
the night I swam naked in silk
moonlight with a woman
in an eggshell Adirondack lake. See,
her form shimmers, her arms
stay silver in the sky's
membrane and our feet
still slur
underwater in dark weed and sand.

Then we drove home wrapped
in stiff towels, skyward
through the mountains, back
into two separate
selves that waxed until we broke
apart. It was a mystery
I see now made of moths,
swarms hooding the windshield as we took
familiar curves, enfolding us
for seconds in one pearl–
white cell.

The highway cleared but still
I don't know what was flecked and
loosened to the air, and what
drives on, knifing
as through skin.

The Birds of Ireland

1 GREAT HATRED, LITTLE ROOM

Broke, in my mother's country
where there are no woods,
we love birds *ssshh* each other
in the dark when the landlord
knocks. "The Irish
have strong roots," declared
some woman in a book
decked out in cartoon
Elizabethan cloak & boots
and I believe her. Birds
are everywhere—not just
the dirt breeders New Yorkers
curse, but swans—muddy, beating
eerie rounds a far cry
from mythology—still, swans
whose cries after a sleepless
night I pretend wake me
to find us reconciled—naked
& pink in our tiny flat
with the stove burners on.

When I walk out wind
cakes spit in my scarved throat
and caws & honks rise from the
Lee tide like bitter–
ness of forests
sheared by foreign
armies fearing night,
reproaches against
history, against husbands
who lay simpering, drunk
stiff as gloves.

2 Lapis Lazuli

You struggle on your back, trying
to break 115. I read translations

from the Japanese and watch your legs pump
imaginary petals. Your hip bone pops

as you row an imaginary boat.
You've come to rescue me, adrift, at home.

I should exercise too, you huff. I discover
I'd been living alone in squalor.

The room refines itself, expending immense effort.
Gates & trapdoors open in thin air.

You take a break. "Hollow, awhirl,
the inside of a vast expanding pearl…"

"What's that you say?" you pivot, offering
a carrot, and from dark inside me

a moth darts into light
and ignites, silently.

3 A Cigarette for Yeats

A bachelor and shy, he
strung luxurious rhymes
across his benefactress's
ormula writing table,
and reclined, puffing
a hand–rolled silk
cigarette between
each line composed.

Once, his weak gaze
pierced the gallow–

glass slit in Lady Gregory's
high tower—and he glimpsed
cygnet wings clip by so fast
from that day on
he snipped
each cigarette in half.

4 AND THIS IS HOW I WOKE

Behind our flat the head of a water pump
just tops the weeds: a shrine
of rust in ten square feet of growth.
No one goes there. Our window
faces the outer wall of stone. I know,
a century ago, anonymous,
ill–paid hands fitted the stones, gapped and irregular,
with nothing but hand tools, mud, and ladders,
into that cliff.

I fall asleep
alone, mid–afternoon.
Then I hear
weeds plunging over the dead
hand pump and see
a stream
striking a teaspoon
that turns the water
into an oval flame.

5 THE LIGHT OF EVENING

    Frost
cakes the window
    and beyond
the moon
    seals the river
in a pane of ice.

How easy to imagine
      that the drowned
can go no further:
      that their eyes
the color of river
      watch
the same moon mine do.

When I turn
      to the living
room again
      and hear
wind screech
      in the tiny chimney
I listen to them
      reassemble:
fingers like mine
      arms stuck
akimbo, unable
      to continue
some imagined
      journey seaward—
frozen
      below the ice
plateau where storm
      sounds to reawakened
ears like *hum*
      solitude, home.

Drinking alone
      what wouldn't I
give now
      to hear them speak,
and so I steal
      downstairs,
skid down the bank
      boots first,
rasp *knife*
      into the mouths
heels score
      into the ice

hoping to hear the echo:
>   *safe*
if.
I sprawl
on the raw slab
>   to coax them—
boat, I call
>   the thread
of mucus
>   fastened
to the ice.
>   What can I say
to charm one
>   spasm of the past
from numb lips? *Luster*
>   I blabber,
gin, as blood drains
>   from my palms
& kneecaps
>   *Rumanian women,*
the roof of a cow's mouth.

6 CHOICE AND CHANCE

"What are we doing here,"
>   you hiss
and smack the pillow—
>   "squeezing our last
dime to emigrate
>   backward?"

I claw the blankets off,
>   stamp through creaking dark
and crack
>   with a sharp elbow to the wall
the ear
>   I imagine pressed
to eavesdrop murder.
>   Hunched over cold punch,
I mole fists deep

        in my boxer shorts
and watch
        dawn film
the flotsam
        grudged to this cheap flat
with gloss.
        "See how I've suffered,"
busks the celery dish.
        "We are more real
than you," teases
        the cracked posset cup.

But your name, *Gagné,*
        is French, not
Irish and it means
        "to win."
You rise, dismiss
        apologies
and navigate with ease
        the clumps of
clothes and frosted
        furniture,
to fry
        a glutinous hunk
of pork, nicked
        from a pantry niche
I did not know exists.

CODA: TO A SHADE

Last night he woke me
the only way dead poets can: by fright.

Long released from civil war, magic,
tower in Galway & his lust,

only his weak eyes showed the strain it took
not to dissolve—to stay so long distinct

from the unbodied rage
of all defeated gravities,

and to recognize Yanks, sober,
squatting in his Ireland, in love.

New Age

In the airport bar, an English traveller
in ratty tweed fingered my beer and revealed
the mystery of water. How it is two
energies, and if you break the strong
covalent bond, the power of a kidneyful
could light Cleveland. His friend cracked it,
he said. "In six months the atomic age
will end." The discoverer lives in Ohio,
same as me, and for ten years
after dropping out of high school
he stilled and oscillated water and now
molecules open easy as a child turning
a knob. I liked my drinking buddy; his
was the first science that made sense, and so
I offered him a beer and said that James
Wright once called Ohio "Beautiful River."
"You see," he cried, "We'll need a poet
for the new age, the way your Whitman
whistled in the age of steam." It could
be me, he said, grasping my arm—so few
knew the secret—already the Pentagon
had tried to snuff the genius and Japanese
mobsters cruised Columbus in a limo
with $500 million cash.
I'd like being poet of the age—
the true Age of Aquarius. Who,
eking a living in a dead steel town,
wouldn't? I've dreamt of clear water,
dolphins, bodies shimmering in moonlit falls,
but truth is I was in flight from my own
crazed chemicals boiling to explode
for the wife of a nephrologist
who built a mansion on a lake
then broke down, wept
that he loved his nurse more than
his life. Then the wife left me.

The flight was five hours late by now
but there was never time to tell all this
and anyway I began to think
that being Whitman might be what I needed.
What did it matter that I was small,
sparkless as a matchstick splintered?
That the booze I dialysized by nature every night
left me a puddling mute? When my gay,
ex–Jesuit alcoholic shrink typed me
a list of local de–tox centers, shrugging,
"We are all pulled, slowly or less, down,"
I fled, made it as far as the Newark
airport bar—and here, cheap and cheer–
ful, blossomed a new age. I could become
large, contain multitudes—and pull
myself together as the England
I was bound for once bound the unknown
earth by water. Only we few,
we blessed, believed and understood
and if science scoffed, our faith
would whet revenge on all the tyrant
high school physics teachers and their prize
pupils who plugged on to become
doctors greedy to live only their own
deadening lives forever. Faith, it took.
The genius of the new age was called
Stanley Meyer, confided my new friend.
His own name, printed on a card, read L.
Houlihan, Scientist. We shook hands on it.
I bought another round. "A New Science
of Christ," he prophesized. "All things
broken, then bound again; the kingdom
here, now—no one sees." The secret
of water was in The Book of Job
for all to see but only Stanley Meyer
from Ohio found it. "When the world
shatters, then unbind the waters." That's
genius—to surface from one's murky self,
to be, alone, anywhere, *what is,* to whisper
light as foam, over and over until words
break and reform stranding each God–

fresh hyroglyph in a hiss of uttering.
Yes, I thought, that's it—I'm not Whitman;
I've no voice to birth new worlds—
I'm Job: tight-lipped, obedient, though stripped
of wife, kine, children. Like him,
I circle, dizzy, a dead core, bound
by memory and cannot break free.
I've been abroad six months now, and I fear
the Feds or Japs have nailed Meyer,
or perhaps he never had, or just mislaid
the secret of the age of water. Still,
there's my friend, who flew home happily
to wait. Sometimes, besotted, drenched with rain,
I think of Houlihan and all that power.

Mazembé

Across a decade and lost distances
I remember Lubumbashi and the night
we played Mazembé on a blacktop
under a full moon. Sharp shadows
and the feel of the balloon-warped
basketball, the panting, smacks—
they're with me here in the white room
where mind and heart knit silently.
Mazembé: Swahili for Bulldozer,
the class of the Katanga circuit,
five hulks of six foot sculpted
raw in copper mines, plus Vedette,
the star, a waiter at the Greek
Club with a gold tooth and a manic
will to drive no way but right.

We were three Peace Corps brats, a diamond
smuggler and the cultural attaché,
rumored a spy. But to Mazembé
and the crowd—a swaying, three-deep
out-of-bounds line, we were
Les Americains—Les
because the only ones they'd seen,
and despite our cons and gaudy
tank-tops some doubted we were real
since, but for me, we looked Zairois:

Reggie, a slick 6'2" point guard
who logged pine time at Duke; Mike,
the Georgia ex-tackle; Clarence,
with great wheels and a schizo
passport; Godfrey—avuncular,
40—the first black player ever
in the SEC—once he was
jackknifed by a redneck fan
and he showed us the new moon scar

on his smooth paunch; and me—I too
existed then—a stick 6'3"
160 after lunch, with
a high school jump shot that lured
Coach "Diamond Jim" Valvano
to weaken my knees with hope
of stardom, a new father,
and 800 bucks from Bucknell U;
that phone call marked the peak
of my American career.

In Lubumbashi I was 24,
real to the touch, visible
to myself, not merely to the eyes
that peer pearl blank or curious
through the lead glass portal.
I was in love and twice I lay
awake all night with happiness.

And though the next ten years locked
her and me in tiny furnished
rooms that buzz now round my skull,
looping a home that vanished when
we tried the door, those first
nights promised sleep and the long
full rainbow pattern of a life.

Mazembé trained barefoot and chanted
at halftimes. They tore up
local comp, trouncing the gang
of college kids I coached (I learned
French in huddles—my French
for pick was pique; shoot was shooté
with a hand flip) until finally
I put myself in, missed three prayers
and went red when the jeer msungu
est parresseur was translated—
"the white guy's lazy." Crazed
for revenge I got myself traded
for two pairs of tire–retread
sneakers and a new Dr. J.

ABA ball. But even
the ivory the Belgian priest
who bought me smuggled to build
a gym and skim the best toughs off
the Lubumbashi streets wasn't
enough to beat Mazembé—they
snapped the full court press I chalked
my thugs through, turning the game
into a lay–up drill.
                  And so
the Americans was my own idea.

In Lubumbashi American
meant TESL and sipping rob–roys
at the Consulate. It meant
riding big red Chinese bikes
and wearing jeans and beads.
But being in love, I loved the thing
I was. Each shard, each caricature
of us seemed laughable and precious—
I loved our franglais and the way
we ambled with bulging backpacks
through the streets. I paced
before my frosh declaiming:
"I celebrate MYSELF, and sing
MYSELF" flinging my hands worldward
as they smirked and murmured in mock–trance
whit–man whit–man. The days fit
snug to nights, amazing to me
now, drifting in shades, among
undulating shapes: smoke coils,
lanteen panels, and each flame
shadow tingling to the touch.

That night under strange stars
and swelling moon we high–fived,
juked and showboated our warm–ups.
It had been hard getting the guys up:
I'd nagged Mike, and bribed Reggie
from his bush post two days off
by promising a night–life

that earned this town the name "Evil
Elizabethville." Godfrey was skittish
being seen with Clarence, and Clarence
was nervous being seen. But though
we'd never even seen each other
play, we fanned to the opening
jump ball circle like one hand
opening.
          The pleasure was talking
trash, was being on this black
paved rectangle in Africa
at home. The pleasure was sadness
we were only five who'd been
an entire world. And she was there.

Last night I dreamt her as she was
that night: small ringless hands, bright
nimbus of dark hair, her aura
of grace and mockery as she reached,
bent slightly from a waist
Vallejo would call "spiritual"
to snatch the towel I'd flung.
These nightmares, bright as ointment,
flay me to viscera and when the white-
smocked resident scrapes a folding chair
closer to mine my nerves unsheath:
any of a billion clock ticks—
each a separate, recurring
incarnation—splinters to life:
licking her arched foot after
a bee sting; sliding naked down
a summer slope; last night it was
the towel's frayed wings opening
toward her hands, her hands opening
a chasm: the still night, Vedette,
Mazembé, and the close-packed crowd.

Reggie sparked first; he blurred past
midcourt pressure, froze, then
performed a feat never before
witnessed: he dribbled through his legs

and dished to Clarence slicing in.
The crowd gaped, a high voice keened
rej–jie, and we five heard
a weird echo of electric
hoards chanting, REG–GIE, REG–GIE
to the Bronx sky. But this was Katanga:
forbidden name, echoing recent
slaughter. Katanga, where Tshombé
was uncrowned king, where Lumumba,
half–dead, grovelling, was made to eat
his constitution. Katanga,
where rebels with fetishes strong enough
to bend Mobutu's rifles swept
out of the bush to take Kolwesi;
where government troops shot whites
before fleeing, to force the U.N.
mercenaries to fight. These were the names,
the rumors murmured over drinks
at the Macreese, Karavia, the Park,
the velvet, malachite–glitzed lounges
where ex–pats, wrung to sallow wraiths,
hung on. But this night, we were myth—
Rej–jie was fetisheur; the rock
flowed silver between charmed
forms: our charged, accomplishment
bodies—jump shot, slash
and drive; even before my second
wind we pulled out to a 10–2 lead.

Anger and joy came easily
those days, particles knotting,
bursting, but that night
for the first time I saw rage
contained. Vedette, his face tight
as a V, spun baseline right,
head faked, and elbowed Mike in the gut.
Mike gagged, doubled, then spluttered
at the ref, "il a presque moi
TUE!" No call. I had to waltz
Godfrey away when the star flashed
the same grin he served with

cappucino and I saw then what
Mazembé wanted from this game.
They ran straight lanes, give–and–go's,
and a funky weave cribbed out of
Naismith's guide. Their antique
set shots looked like trophies
spasming but they clawed
each board, and sniffed our shorts on D;
and at the half, the score was tied.

Jack Sullivan, crew–cut maniac
coach of Fordham Prep, once slapped
me at half–time for saying "Fuck."
I should have walked, or smacked him,
but I sat, red–faced, feeling the sting
numb my cheek and will until
it seemed I peered at lockers
and shifting eyes of eleven boys,
till then my team, from a great
distance. Sometimes when I am
reached into and grabbed
I am that boy. Jack loved us—
so he said—for this we called him
bent and snickered when he bawled
after each loss. To wring
love out of flesh, to make
it come—reach in with hands—
just try. That's how it was
the night I breathe hard now
to keep from entering—from swallowing
me—the night last month she shivered
in moonlight, one hand on her stung
cheek, the other gesturing
from her breasts, "You just
dissolved our love."

"Positive Imaging," whispers
the owl–faced senior therapist,
zinging my head with Prozac,
sedatives. "Write pictures

of the good; the mind is a made
place, can be re–made like this."

And so I float towards Africa,
full moon, and the dense, swaying crowd.
Starting the second half I felt
the touch: Reggie sensed it, fed me
in the corner, at the top
of the key, deep low post. I was un–
conscious, zoned, untouchable—
as when, a boy, alone in winter
parks, I'd shoot till my paws
bled—it was the cure for being
me—I was West, Havlicek—
not a mute scarlet lightbulb
pulsing against a slap.
                        The touch—
the hoop was a glazed wafer
and my body, slight as a bow,
chin tilted, elbow cocked,
flickered in night air.
                        The touch—
echoed in words, and words
only a faint omen for the way
the self, supple as a tongue,
speaks and is heard.
                        Lovers,
we felt it, ached after it,
                        fading.
Touch: to glide and turn fishlike
in the world, inside
the other—a new being, translucent
rose globe unbound by skin.

It doesn't last, even a night.
The hands grope, the mind shrinks
to a pea in fog, until in
moonlight last month when she reached
into me finally I was
not there—I was the boy
unmoored from home and he lashed back.

The rest of the game's a dream
of struggling through swaths
of cotton—Mazembé swarming, our limbs
gone spidery. We kept it close
on instinct and cheap fouls, hobbling
on fresh blisters, sucking wind.
I dogged Vedette—this man who flamed
into himself and into us
between flaked lines, then
vanished in a maze
of gestures, smiles, and nods.

From the state the shrinks call
clinical depression, but which
Catullus knew as "a paralysis
which creeps from limb to limb,
driving all former laughter
from the heart," an eerie place
Bird found, suddenly half out
of his magnificent self while pain
seared the branches of his back,
I cling to the night against Mazembé
and to three thousand nights that wove
a canopy ripped when my own
palm—the hand belonging to the man
I must be now—struck her face.

I recall the ease, the sweet
exhaustion and the beer, strangers
pumping my hand, the scorekeeper
waving crinkled looseleaf proof
that this night did take place. "Ah,
Mazembé yes, too much," he sighed.
"But tonight, Philippe,
tonight you were the chef."

Single Flat

Windows thrust out to a sheer drop barbed with pine twigs,
    rugs ticklish with kitty litter and spilt seed,

these are the rooms I keep, that keep me
    alive and awake after breaking

or bending like wire hangers or afternoon light.
    Rooms where I stroke myself

in the shape of a cat, where I fence spider plants
    and bark at the bleeding tea: rooms

high as fierce seas yet so still
    breath massages a candleflame;

knobs that harrumph to sign checks; walls
    that relax to the texture of honeyed soup;

rooms of salt water, of mink–oiled goat–skin drums;
    vegetable rooms, rooms of stealth;

rooms I lower my mind's
    body into as into a steaming bath,

if I sing, if I bang chairs and bully your stove,
    will you speak to me

rooms? Will we wink over milk at the nights
    we licked pills and woke stepping on dead

horseshoe crabs? Outside the young fiends
    key my car and spray paint the lawn

chartreuse X and when I lure anyone up
    from the bars and the offices, up

groaning steep cornices runed with hairballs and lint,

        you ignite the flesh I want to caress

my sleep, and guide my left hand to the pulse
        of its own vanishing, pulse

I love finally now for your sake, though my hand
        recoils as if it had touched a bat.

I don't want to hear banshees in the wheezing hoover;
        I do not believe you are made of tenants' bones;

I know you don't mean to spin; I know you will stop
        corkscrewing light through my brain when I say *three*.

To Catullus

    and as I once was whole, make me now whole again.

Friend, piss–yellow ghost, peacock,
like you, like your brother
beautiful excrescences Villon
and Yeats, I only wanted
to marry my mother and be rocked
in her foam–bright arms
between a toy world and oblivion.

Sometimes sinking to sleep I think
you're with me in her mansion by a lake
and slowly the house
unmoors from grass and glides
down the long slope and slides in.
She is our Lesbia, she chose
this house with its patrician
lord instead of us
to soothe her since she knew
she had but the one life. With you
I rush—penniless
mad scarecrow—through the wind;
I want those scars—my eyes—to un–
knit till my body is sky
blue. I want to unspool. To be
a cloud of gnats
licking her ears.
                Hearing
you coo love, hearing
poor, drunk Herrick
guzzle fate, and
James Wright, who called you
fire, bleed into the slit
of his dead river, I want
to gulp from my quick veins and let
the thin, numb lightning shoot down

my cigarette arm. Sinking to sleep
while eels and stingrays gleam,
if I could pry one window—
let bright amniotic water
swirl, even in dream, just once,
into my doll–red mouth,
we could be whole—stop
rocking and crooning, our mouths
pressed yearning—now
to the world, now to
a sea–dark pane we cloud with breath—
possible or not, possible
or not.
Stay with me. Let go.

Letter to Ireland

from: Roger Casement
to: Agnes Newman

       July 12, 1903, Ibiaku

My dear sister,

So you think your man John Redmond
will redeem the Chief? But Parnell lives
his dream beyond his end—he is
more real as shadowy Dead King
than when he muddled speeches in Mayo.
Alive, how out of place he seemed—
stone–faced ascendancy do–gooder
stilting clichés from such height he drove
rain into the upturned faces of his
bovine worshippers. Remember him
saying Tom Kettle's name would be
a household word? But I've chewed Ireland's
cud long enough among the flies
of Leopoldsville—Sir Roger Casement,
His Majesty's Vice–Consul—presiding
as the pageantry of suffering awes
new upturned faces.
And so I pocketed your letter,
trudged east a hundred miles to answer
here. Lost in the sun's glare, I dreamed
I'd sip palm wine on the bank
of a great sourceless river, write
from deep within some nameless
well of blood. But here
turns out to be somewhere
made up—some place I wanted to call
Eden—at least garden—where the ice
emerald that scorched my soul at birth
with penal laws, famine, orange drums

would refract into the infinite
hues of palm wine, leaf, and sky.

Here, yesterday,
a man feathered like a bird
wept in my arms. He was rank
with blood and palm oil and I confess
the cold bile missionaries take
for righteousness rose in my throat.
Then I heard, between his sobs,
my name—last heard 20 years ago—
Monafuma—and I knew this place
I wanted to be nowhere
was Ibiaku, where once a feathered chief
placed raw meat on the quivering tongue
of the young adventurer I was—
first white man he had ever seen—
saying *take, Monafuma.* And I knew
the rumors of a great massacre
by whites were true.

Nina, you must think I don't remember—
being a small boy—spitting
at the frosted oaks where papist waifs
barbed shrikes—how we unhooked
and buried with all righteous hate
their bloody offense to the pure air
of Ulster's winter. Yesterday
as my chief's son scorched my mind
with images of devastation I saw
the arch of that spit flame
to a torched beehive launched
by my own kin
in a barrage of fire—and it burst
upon me for the first time
who I was—as if before I
hadn't known even the simplest things—
why I speak English or what
love feels like. Nina,
Rory I am, here Monafuma—
brother to these also dispossessed.

The New Life

When Father, murderous,
leaned over me in the pew and hissed
at Mother, *After Mass,* Christ
was a fish
twisting in my stomach.

The sky is *Hollowéd*, I pled, and *blesséd
the bruised fruit*, but caught
with my scared eye
only the intricate relief
of figures carved
in torture
in lamplight.

What I'd pray now
to Christ, to you
my love and to your
two boys drowning
toward a father
thrashing undersea
is

*Let there be one,
one life, and that
separate and carved
like a wood bead.*

I would not father,
even to knead
the salt–sweet
infant skin,

even if love, to last, must strain
flesh thongs until
a child gleams, lashes
free, even if

to murder.

You are the last. I
love you. And we
are thonged invisibly
to separate lives
constricting now, like two
parched spines, unless

we break
together in green darkness

to be the sole
ribbed
feather printed
in sea stone.

NOTES

The Casement Letters

Sir Roger Casement (1864–1916) arrived in the Congo in 1884 to work on the first railroad under the supervision of Henry Morton Stanley. Later, he became British Vice-Consul to the Belgian Congo. In 1904 he wrote "The Congo Report," a detailed account of his independent investigations into the conditions of the native people as he observed them on a journey up the Congo River.

In 1916, Casement was tried and convicted of high treason for his part in the Easter Rebellion. During and after his trial, diaries dated 1903–1904, purportedly in Casement's hand, were circulated secretly by the British Foreign Minister to counter petitions for clemency put forward by prominent citizens in England and America. "The Black Diaries," as they were called, gave evidence of homosexual encounters. Casement was hanged August 3, 1916.

Korzeniowski is of course Joseph Conrad, who met Casement on the novelist's famous journey to the Congo. "Letter to Photograph" paraphrases some of Conrad's written comments about the meeting.

Charles Stewart Parnell (1829–1892) led the Irish Parliamentary Party from 1876 until a scandel involving Parnell and the wife of another M.P. split the party in 1891. He was known as "The Chief" and "The Uncrowned King of Ireland." John Redmond reunited the I.P.P. in 1901.

It is a custom for Irish Catholic children to hunt wrens on St. Stephan's Day and ornament them as if for a funeral.

Wiretap

In 1966, Alice Crimmons was tried and convicted of murder after the deaths of her two children, Eddie, nine years old, and Alice, age six. One key witness was the Queens County Coroner, Harold Goldin, who testified that the deaths occurred before 2:00 A.M., an hour before

Alice claimed to have seen both children. *The Alice Crimmons Case*, by Kenneth Gross, was published by Bantam Books in 1974.

THE ARRIVAL OF THE QUEEN OF SHEBA (IN GALWAY)

The title come from the Irish traditional music group De Danaan's arrangement of Handel's "The Arrival of the Queen of Sheba."

The baseball players, Jerry Koosman, Tom Seaver, Ed Kranepool, and Bud Harrelson played for "The Miracle Mets" of 1969; while Sandy Koufax, Jackie Robinson, and Gil Hodges (who managed the '69 Mets) played for the Brooklyn Dodgers of the '40's and '50's. Walter O'Malley, the Dodgers' owner, moved the team to Los Angeles in 1956. Cletus (Clete) Boyer played third for the Yankees of the '60's.

THE DREAM MY FATHER RADIOS

Herb Score (b.1933) pitched for the Cleveland Indians from 1955–1962. In his second year, he was struck in the face by a line drive. He never fully recovered.

Wrong–Way Corrigan left New York on route to California in 1937, but landed his twin–engine plane in Kerry, Ireland.

Joe Louis (1914–1983) was knocked out by Max Schmelling in 1936.

LETTER TO AMERICA

The Simbas, a rebel group opposed to the government of President Joseph Mobutu, occupied Ibiaku in 1964, taking three hundred Belgian, American, and Congolese hostages before being defeated by a combined force of Belgian and American troops. General Olenga was their military leader.

Mai means 'water' in Swahili and Lingala. Simba soldiers believed that the chant would turn enemy bullets to water.

A NOTE ABOUT THE AUTHOR

Philip Brady was born in New York City and received a B.A. from Bucknell and Masters degrees from the University of Delaware and San Fransisco State University. He received a Ph.D in English from SUNY Binghamton in 1990. He has taught at University College Cork in Ireland, and, as a Peace Corps Volunteer, at the University of Lubumbashi in Zaire. Currently, he is Associate Professor of English and Creative Writing at Youngstown State University, where he directs the Poetry Center.